I Am Kind.
I Do Not BULLY!

My Amazing Toddler
Behavioral Series

An Affirmation-Themed Toddler
Book About Not Bullying (Ages 2-4)

By

Suzanne T. Christian

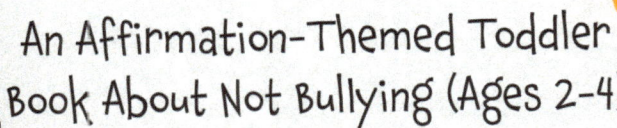

TWO RAVENS
BOOKS

Two Little Ravens
CHILDREN'S NON-FICTION BOOKS

Paperback Edition: 9781964202501
Hardcover Edition: 9781964202518
Digital Edition: 9781964202525

Published in the United States by Two Ravens Books LLC,
254 Chapman Rd, Ste 209, Newark DE 19702

'Expand the mind, free the imagination, one title at a time.'
www.tworavensbooks.com

Welcome to

"I Am Kind. I Do Not Bully!"

This book is a delightful collection of easy-to-understand affirmations for young children.

As you read together, your child will learn the power of kindness, gentle words, and empathy. Each page features vivid illustrations and relatable scenarios that encourage caring interactions.

By revisiting this book regularly, you'll harness the proven teaching power of repetition, helping your child gradually adopt more positive behaviors.

Get ready to embark on a joyful journey filled with emotional growth, understanding, and plenty of fun with your toddler!

Suzanne T. Christian

When I feel angry,
I count to 5.
I do not bully!

Using kind words makes everyone smile.

Using my words helps me show my feelings.

I ask for a turn instead of grabbing.

If I hurt someone,
I say "I'm sorry".
I do not bully!

I like giving big smiles,
Not pushes.

I tell grown-ups when
I'm mad or sad.

I share crayons so we
can color together.
I do not bully!

I use a calm voice
even when I'm angry.

I wait my turn like
a patient penguin;
I do not bully!

When I feel angry, I take a deep breath and clap my hands.

Hugs are better than hits— way better!

If I don't win, I say,
'Good job!'
and try again.
I do not bully!

Being kind makes me
feel like a superhero!

I love to laugh
with friends,
not laugh at them.

I am kind, even when I feel sad.

I use gentle hands
and gentle words.
I do not bully!

I stomp my feet on the floor, not on my friends.

Kindness grows bigger
when I share it.
I do not bully!

When a friend
won't let me play,
I tell a grown-up.
I do not bully!

I Am Kind.
I Do Not
BULLY!
The End!

My Amazing Toddler Behavioral Series

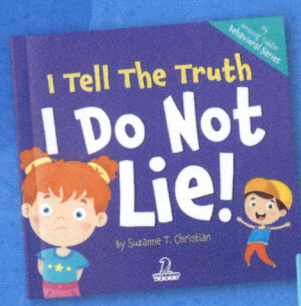

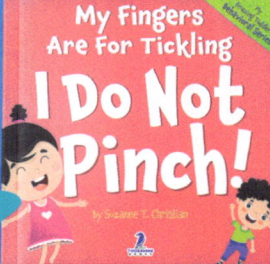

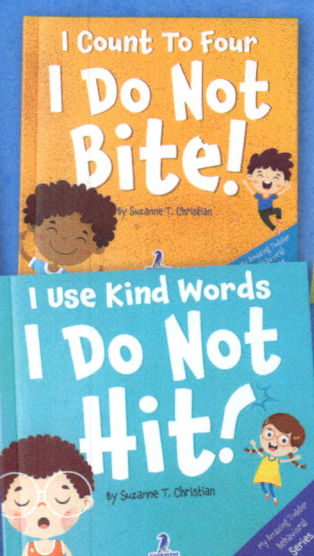

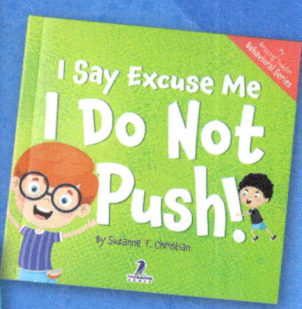

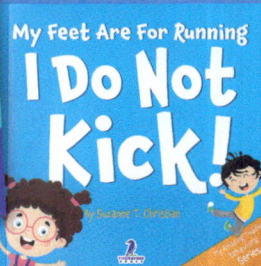

Check Out
Suzanne T. Christian's beloved series
'My Amazing Toddler Behavioral Series'.
Young readers are sure to enjoy!

Two Little Ravens
CHILDREN'S NON-FICTION BOOKS

Dear Amazing Reader,

Thank you for diving into **I Am Kind. I Do Not Bully!** with me. If this book touched your heart or made a difference for a young reader, I'd be grateful if you could share your thoughts in a review. Your feedback inspires my future work and helps others discover the magic within these pages.

I'd love to hear from you directly if you have suggestions or ideas for improving the book. Please feel free to reach out to me at suzanne.christian@tworavensbooks.com. Your voice counts, and I cherish it deeply.

With heartfelt gratitude,